STATE
OF AFFAIRS:
NATIVE AMERICANS
IN THE 21ST CENTURY

PRESERVING THEIR
HERITAGE

TAMMY GAGNE

Mitchell Lane
PUBLISHERS

P.O. Box 196
Hockessin, Delaware 19707
Visit us on the web: www.mitchelllane.com
Comments? Email us: mitchelllane@mitchelllane.com

STATE
OF AFFAIRS:
NATIVE AMERICANS
IN THE 21st CENTURY

Preserving Their Heritage
Native Americans and the Government
Native American Industry in Contemporary America
Life on the Reservations

Printing   1   2   3   4   5   6   7   8   9

Library of Congress
Cataloging-in-Publication Data Applied For

PUBLISHER'S NOTE: The facts on which the story
in this book is based have been thoroughly
researched. Documentation of such research
can be found on page 44. While every possible
effort has been made to ensure accuracy, the
publisher will not assume liability for damages
caused by inaccuracies in the data, and
makes no warranty on the accuracy of the
information contained herein.

eBook ISBN: 9781612285023

ABOUT THE AUTHOR:
Tammy Gagne has written numerous books for
adults and children, including *A Kid's Guide
to the Voting Process* and *The Power of the
States* for Mitchell Lane Publishers. She counts
American history and civics among her many
interests. She resides in northern New England
with her husband and son. One of her favorite
pastimes is visiting schools to speak to kids
about the writing process.

PLB

CONTENTS

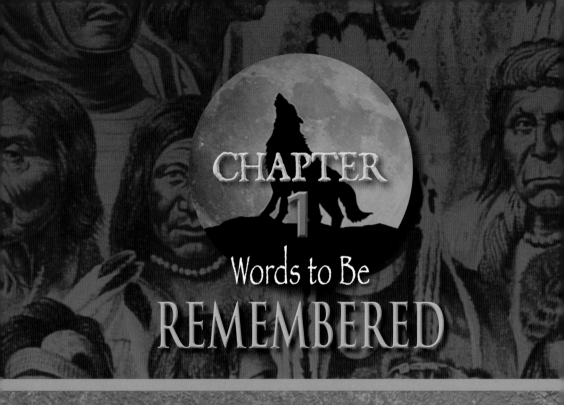

CHAPTER 1

Words to Be

REMEMBERED

The powwow begins with the beating of the drums. A large crowd has gathered to see the Native American chiefs and elders make their big entrance. They wear brightly colored outfits with beautiful beadwork and large feathers. They parade in together, forming a line so that each one of them can be seen. Next to enter are the dancers. Many of them have won contests at some of the biggest events around the country. The audience is made up of many Native Americans. After all, the powwow is a big part of their heritage. It is an opportunity to celebrate all that they believe in and hold dear. But there are others in the crowd as well. People have come from both near and far to learn about this way of life. And in the tradition of their ancestors, the Native Americans welcome them all.

The United States has a vast history that began long before the founding fathers even gave our country its name. Spanish explorer Christopher Columbus arrived in North America in 1492. Although he is often said to have discovered the Americas at

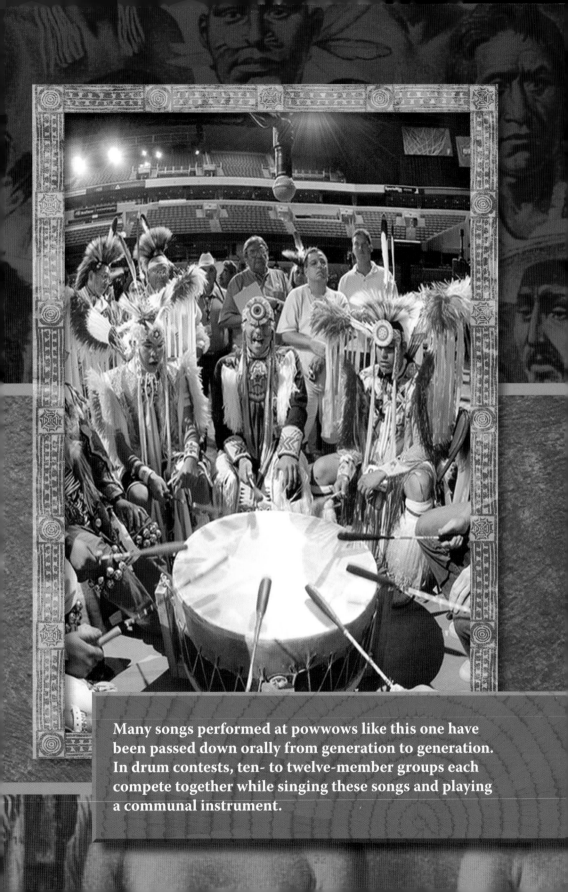

Many songs performed at powwows like this one have been passed down orally from generation to generation. In drum contests, ten- to twelve-member groups each compete together while singing these songs and playing a communal instrument.

Many people mistakenly think of the Pilgrims as the first settlers of the land now called the United States. Long before these Europeans arrived on American shores, however, Native Americans lived here. They are the oldest known inhabitants of North America.

this time, Norsemen had in fact landed here almost five hundred years earlier. During the seventeenth century, the first British colonies were established, and the United States became an independent country with the American Revolution over 150 years later. Since that time, our history has been shaped by people of various ethnicities. Many Americans have come to the United States from faraway places. Modern America has developed as a result of the blending of these many cultures.

While historians debate about who discovered America, the fact that the land was already settled when the various Europeans arrived is often overlooked. Native Americans, sometimes called American Indians, are the oldest known inhabitants of North America. Unlike most other cultures, this group does not consist of a single people. Hundreds of different Native American tribes lived throughout the continent long before the first European settlers arrived. Many of these tribes still exist today. They share many traits, but each one has its own distinct culture with its

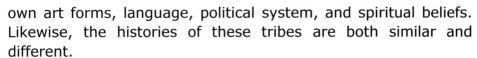

own art forms, language, political system, and spiritual beliefs. Likewise, the histories of these tribes are both similar and different.

Modern history is recorded each and every day by professional writers and even regular people. When something happens today, chances are good that someone is nearby with a video camera to document the event. Many times these recording devices are even housed in cell phones. Hundreds of years ago this technology didn't exist. Back then, history was recorded on parchment with quill pens—most history, that is.

A large amount of Native American history was never written down at all. Instead, the stories were passed down over generations. One might assume that this storytelling was done because early tribes lacked the tools to create history books. While this is partly true, it is important to understand that storytelling was—and still is—a respected part of Native American culture. Tribe elders used storytelling as a way to teach their younger members about their history, religion, and even medicine.

One problem with this way of relaying history is that children had to continue the tradition as adults in order for the stories to survive for future generations. The languages of some tribes didn't even have written forms. Navajo, for example, was strictly an oral language until the US government began documenting it during the middle of the nineteenth century.[1]

Sadly, many Native American children didn't live long enough to pass on their tribes' stories. Among the things that European settlers brought with them to North America were diseases like measles, scarlet fever, and smallpox. These deadly illnesses took the lives of countless Native Americans, wiping out many small tribes entirely. Because Europeans had already been exposed to these diseases for hundreds of years, they possessed immunity that the Native Americans lacked.

As time passed, some Native Americans began recording their tribes' histories on paper. Many of these documents are now housed at the National Archives in Washington, DC. The

majority of this information covers the years between 1830 and 1970.[2] It only includes Native Americans who were part of federally recognized tribes, however.

As technology improved, the problem became more complicated. The same equipment that allowed written records to be stored electronically also created distractions from Native American culture. Instead of sitting around a fire telling stories each evening, modern tribes began doing the same things that other Americans were doing. Towards the end of the twentieth century, television, video games, and personal computers became popular new ways of spending time. When Native American elders died, much of their tribes' history was lost along with them.

One of the biggest parts of Native American culture that has been lost is language. By the late 1800s, the United States had forced most Native American tribes to live on reservations. Native American children were then sent to boarding schools

The student body of the Carlisle Indian School, Pennsylvania, 1885

where they were only allowed to speak English. The United States designed this educational program to integrate Native Americans with the rest of the country. The people in charge believed that speaking a single language would help bring Native Americans and white Americans together. In the process, though, many young Native Americans lost an important link to their past.

Since 1997, at least fifty-five Native American languages have disappeared.[3] Dozens more could be lost in the next several years if they aren't preserved and taught to younger people. Of the approximately 125 languages that are left, most are spoken only by older adults. Only about twenty Native American languages are spoken widely by children.

Thankfully, not all Native American history has been lost. A large amount still exists, but recording it must become a top priority if Native American heritage is to be preserved for future generations. George Cornell is the director of the Native American Institute at Michigan State University and a Native American himself. He asserts that it is important to study languages even if they may never be spoken widely again. "All you have to do is ask, 'Why study Latin?'—a language that's been dead for a thousand years—and then you realize how much these Native American languages have to teach us," he explains.[4]

Dr. Greg Anderson is the director of Living Tongues, an organization that records languages from all over the world that are at risk of disappearing. His work with Native American languages focuses on "hotspots"—areas with the largest number of languages that have not been studied and are at risk of dying out. Currently, these areas are in and around the states of Oklahoma and Oregon.

Historically, Oregon had the highest number of Native American languages in the United States for its size. This state has lost many languages, though. As Dr. Anderson points out, "At the time Lewis and Clark arrived in what's now Oregon two hundred years ago, there were fourteen language families, more than in all of Europe combined. Today, only five families of

Linguist Dr. Greg Anderson is the director of the Living Tongues Institute for Endangered Languages. He travels to areas all over the world in search of endangered languages. His goal is to document these languages and keep them from becoming extinct.

languages exist, and most of them have only a handful of speakers."[5]

Just because a language still exists doesn't mean that it is also used regularly. Dr. Anderson shares, "There is only one language family [in Oregon] that has more than a hundred or two hundred speakers, and that's Northern Paiute, in southeastern Oregon, where the elders can still speak it when they get together. For most of the rest of the people there the everyday language is English."[6]

PUTTING IT ON PAPER

In 1849, an officer in the US Army named James H. Simpson published the *Journal of a Military Reconnaissance.* This book included a list of words in Navajo and other Native American languages. Numerous missionaries also worked to put the Navajo language down on paper. They created dictionaries, educational textbooks, and religious guides, all in the Navajo language as they heard it. Unfortunately, each author came up with different spellings for the words. This was extremely confusing for everyone involved.

John Collier, head of Indian Affairs, teamed up with Willard Beatty, the head of Indian Education, during the 1930s to solve this problem. They asked a group of linguists to create a standard Navajo alphabet. The Navajo language includes numerous sounds and tones that are not used in English. By 1939, John Harrington, Oliver LaFarge, William Morgan, and Robert Young had created this new alphabet.

The Navajo people did not welcome the alphabet, however. Perhaps they simply did not want to adopt written language as part of their culture. But the fact that Collier was behind the new writing system probably didn't help. Collier had previously introduced the Navajo Livestock Reduction program, stating that there were too many animals grazing on too little land. His solution was to slaughter the majority of these animals without Navajo consent. This act was devastating to the tribe, as the livestock had both cultural and economic value to the Navajo.

James H. Simpson

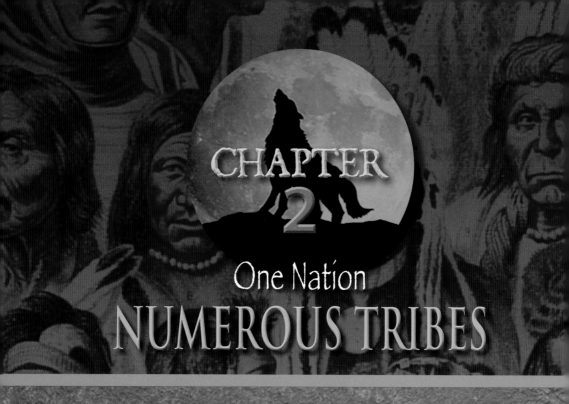

CHAPTER 2

One Nation

NUMEROUS TRIBES

It is impossible to describe Native American culture as a whole, because there are so many different tribes. The Algonquian people alone include more than 500,000 individuals belonging to more than 30 different tribes. The word *Algonquian* is used by linguists to describe not only the similarly named Algonquin tribe, but also numerous other tribes who speak related languages. The Chippewa, Passamaquoddy, Powhatan, and Yurok are all grouped as Algonquian tribes. These tribes are located throughout the country, from California to Maine. Some can also be found in southern parts of Canada.

Native American heritage is preserved in words that many of us use every day. Eight US states got their names from Algonquian tribes: Connecticut, Illinois, Massachusetts, Michigan, Mississippi, Missouri, Wisconsin, and Wyoming. Numerous cities and towns across the country also bear names which originated with Algonquian languages. They include Cheyenne, Wyoming; Miami, Florida; and Milwaukee, Wisconsin. The New York City

The Chippewa tribe inhabited land that is now part of several US states including Michigan, Wisconsin, Minnesota, and North Dakota. This tribe also lived along the shores of Lake Huron and Lake Superior in what is now Ontario, Canada.

borough Manhattan was also named for an Algonquian word meaning "island of many hills."

Many other Algonquian words are now commonly used in the English language as well. Words like moccasin, tomahawk, and wigwam all came from these languages. Not all Algonquian words refer exclusively to Native American culture, however. The list includes names for common animals such as the chipmunk, raccoon, and skunk. The names of plants like the hickory, pecan, and squash also share this etymology.

The variety of climates where Native American tribes live is one reason for the diversity among their cultures. To this day, tribes that make their homes in colder climates have to dress much differently than the tribes living in warmer areas. Likewise, these various tribes once lived in different types of homes. They hunted different animals based on the wildlife that inhabited their region of the country. Even the vegetation in each area has played a part in culture, as it has been used for food, medicine, technology, and even tribal ceremonies.

The major Native American cultural areas in what is now the United States are generally divided into seven regions: the Arctic, the Northwest, California and the Great Basin, the Southwest, the Plains, the Northeast Woodlands, and the Southeast.

Native American tribes living nearby other tribes often shared many customs with each other. Some of this common culture developed from living in the same environment. Other shared customs resulted from tribes borrowing ideas from one another.

Since Alaska is also part of the United States, the history of the Arctic tribes is part of our country's Native American culture as well. The Arctic tribes differ from the others the most due to the harsher climate in their remote location. Alaskan tribes do share traits with other Arctic and Subarctic tribes, however. The kayak, a boat used by the Eskimo tribes, is one example of the Arctic Native American technology that has been preserved in modern America. The Arctic people have always been known for

The kayak is an example of Native American technology that has been preserved and shared with the rest of the United States. Arctic tribes created this boat to help their members stay warm and dry while navigating the cold waters of their region.

their resourcefulness. The design of the kayak reflects this trait. The small opening is just large enough for the passenger, keeping the cold water out of the boat. The structure is also easy to flip upright if a strong wave knocks it over.

Many tribes in both the Arctic and the lower regions were nomadic. The Shawnee, for example, lived across the east from Pennsylvania to the South when Europeans arrived in North America. Today, most Shawnees live in Oklahoma or the Ohio River Valley. Although European arrival was the cause of most of this movement, the Shawnee were nomadic long before colonial times. Each of the Shawnees' environments had an effect on the tribe's culture.

Southeastern tribes like the Choctaw, Muskogee, and the Cherokee performed an interesting ritual involving the "black drink." Brewed from a holly shrub and drank from shells, this dark liquid was so strong that it frequently caused people who consumed it to vomit. These Native Americans believed that the

A black tea made from the holly shrub played a key role in the spiritual rituals of several southeastern Native American tribes. So strong that it often caused vomiting, the drink was used to purify the spirit before important dances, council meetings, or religious ceremonies.

black drink helped to purify their spirits. They would use it before an important event, such as a dance or council meeting.

It seems that tribes also acquired some of their customs through trade. Archaeologists have found evidence of the black drink hundreds of miles away in the ancient city of Cahokia, near what is now St. Louis, Missouri.[1] While the southeastern tribes poured the black drink into shells, Native Americans in this area used ceramic cups instead, but the drink itself appears to be the same. By sharing this custom, the tribes of these two different regions also shared a religious ritual.

Traditional Native American religion is based on belief in spirit powers. In most regions, the majority of these spirits are female. The First Mother, for example, is revered by the Abenaki and Penobscot tribes. The Navajo believe in a similar spirit they call the First Woman. Mother-like spirits are common in numerous other tribes as well and are often linked to corn and other fertile

crops. For the Arctic tribes, however, male spirits were more common. The Moon Man, for example, is said to rule the universe—including the sky, the animals, and the people.

A strong connection between people and nature is part of most Native American cultures. Like the cultures themselves, traditional religion also varies greatly from one group to another. In nearly all tribes, however, the earth, its animals, and even invisible forces such as the wind play important roles. If a singular concept about Native American culture does exist, it is a respect for all living things.

Each animal represents something of value in Native American cultures. Dolphins, for example, are considered good omens among coastal tribes. A person with a sick family member may even go to the ocean to pray to this animal, asking for its protection. Seeing a school of dolphins during fishing season is said to be a sign of a prosperous catch. Native Americans who served in the Navy during World War II have witnessed dolphins acting as protectors. They have reported that dolphins helped save the lives of pilots whose planes were shot down during the war. The animals escorted the pilots all the way to shore to protect them from nearby sharks.[2]

Unlike dolphins, sharks are regarded as bad omens. When they swim too close to shore, they are seen as a warning of an impending natural disaster such as an earthquake or hurricane. Sharks that are discovered in fresh-water rivers are thought to be a sign that severe flooding will occur in the area.

For much of the twentieth century, many Native Americans rejected their own cultures out of fear. Parents worried that embracing traditional beliefs and customs would make life more difficult for their children. A large number of Native Americans living on reservations in the United States were among the poorest people in the country. For this reason, many Native American parents encouraged their children to learn English and take part in modern American society. They thought their kids could create better lives for themselves if they left their traditional ways in the past.

The Warm Springs Indian Reservation in Oregon is just one example of the widespread poverty that is affecting Native Americans today. Reservations across the country are filled with homes in disrepair. Many do not have electricity, running water, or telephones.

The twenty-first century, however, is becoming a time of renewed interest in Native American cultures. Both Native Americans and others are interested in learning more about Native American customs and religions. The growing interest in being green—that is, acting with respect for the environment that we all share—is a prime example of how Native American cultures and modern values are merging.

THE UNBREAKABLE CODE

During World War II, the United States needed a code that could not be cracked by its enemies. The Japanese had numerous English-speaking officers who were able to understand the messages that US soldiers were sending to one another. Even when the information was delivered in code, the enemy always seemed to be able to decipher it before the Americans could gain any ground. They needed a code that couldn't be broken.

A small band of Native Americans answered this important call. A civilian named Phillip Johnston came up with an idea after living among the Navajo people years earlier. He was the son of a Protestant missionary and had grown up on the Navajo reservation. Johnston was one of about only thirty non-Navajo who knew the language fluently. He knew that a code based on this difficult language could be the answer US soldiers needed.

Johnston assembled a group of twenty-nine Navajo men. Birth certificates weren't common in Native American tribes during this time, but it is now known that some of these "men" were as young as fifteen years old. Young and old alike, these new soldiers went through basic training to form a unique US Marine unit known as the Navajo Code Talkers.

The code, which at first consisted of about two hundred words, eventually grew to about six hundred words. This list included Navajo words for animals and other objects that resembled military items. For example, the Navajo word for turtle was used for the word "tank." They also created a substitution alphabet of sorts using Navajo words. In it, the Navajo word for ant stood for the letter A, and so on.[3]

The Navajo code made it possible for some messages to be understood by the proper recipients in just seconds. More importantly, the messages couldn't be deciphered by the enemy. The contributions of the Navajo Code Talkers saved thousands of lives until the war's end in 1945.

CHAPTER 3

Keeping Native American
CULTURES ALIVE

The land on which Native Americans live has always played an important part in their tribes' cultures. A deep respect for the land and the wildlife with which they share it is at the core of most tribes' belief systems. In 1990, Congress directed the National Parks Service (NPS) to conduct a study called *Keepers of the Treasures—Protecting Historic Properties and Cultural Traditions on Indian Lands.* The study's report prompted an important new project: the Tribal Preservation Program. This program receives grants from the US government to help protect the natural resources and cultural traditions of many Native American tribes. It also helps train the people to preserve their lands. By 1996, the NPS, along with the Secretary of the Interior, had approved twelve different tribes to help oversee this ongoing project.[1]

One of the goals of the Tribal Preservation Program is to conduct archaeological surveys of the protected land. These searches have unearthed many artifacts that are now housed in

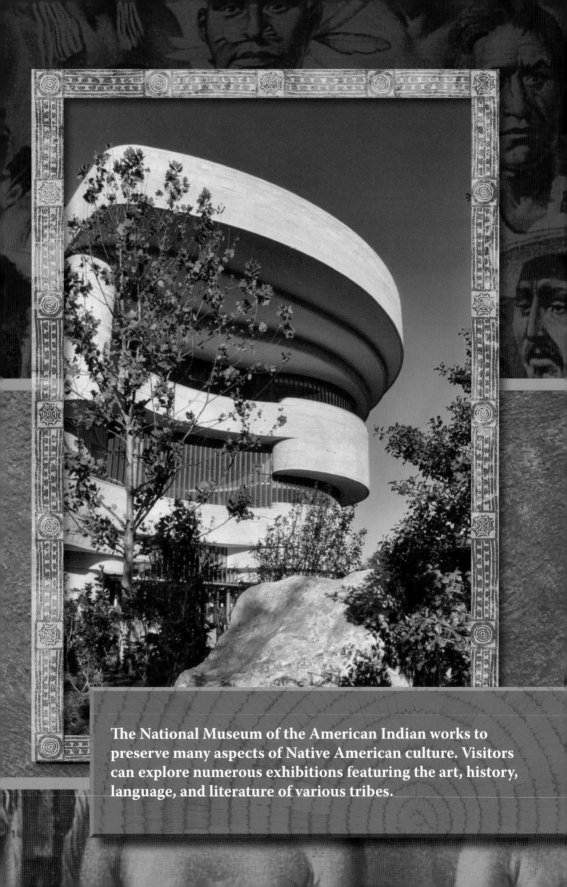

The National Museum of the American Indian works to preserve many aspects of Native American culture. Visitors can explore numerous exhibitions featuring the art, history, language, and literature of various tribes.

According to a Native American legend, Lituya Bay in southeastern Alaska was guarded by a froglike monster and its bear slave. It was said that the bear shook the water's surface, drowning those who traveled through the water. This pipe, which is on display at the NMAI, depicts a canoe that has been struck by the pair's menacing waves.

the National Museum of the American Indian (NMAI). Its collections cover 12,000 years of history from more than 1,200 different cultures—including nearly all the tribes of the United States. In addition to archaeological artifacts, the museum possesses more than 300,000 photos dating as far back as 1860.

Part of the Smithsonian Museum, the NMAI consists of three branches, all of which help preserve the histories and cultures of Native American tribes. The museum on the National Mall in Washington, DC, offers exhibitions, performances, and lectures relating to Native Americans. The George Gustav Heye Center in New York City also offers art exhibitions and performances, as well as educational resources. The Cultural Resources Center in Suitland, Maryland, is home to numerous collections, research facilities, and digital imaging programs. If you can't make it to one of the three NMAI locations, you might be able to attend one of its traveling exhibitions. Information can also be accessed through the NMAI website.

The design of the Cultural Resources Center building is symbolic in many ways. Like historic Native American architecture, the entry is on the east side. Many Native American peoples believed that opening the door to the morning sun meant receiving good blessings. The building creates a strong connection to the environment. The colors and landscaping are simple, blending with the outdoors. Windows and skylights allow large amounts of natural light inside. Even the roof of the building seems to be inspired by nature. To some, its curved roof may look a bit like a nautilus shell; to others it might resemble a pine cone.

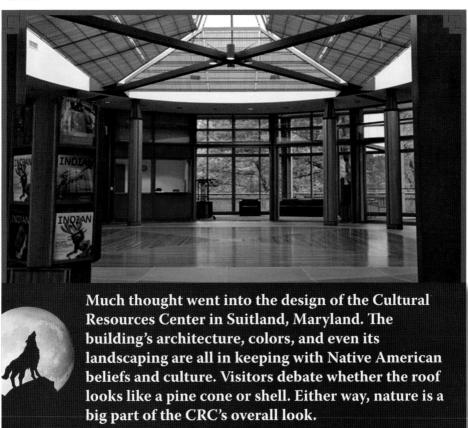

Much thought went into the design of the Cultural Resources Center in Suitland, Maryland. The building's architecture, colors, and even its landscaping are all in keeping with Native American beliefs and culture. Visitors debate whether the roof looks like a pine cone or shell. Either way, nature is a big part of the CRC's overall look.

Quite a few smaller Native American museums and cultural centers can be found across the United States. Many groups hold celebrations called powwows in which Native Americans come together to celebrate their shared cultures. The people sing songs their ancestors sang hundreds of years ago. Drums provide the beats for traditional dances.

Dances are typically performed by either all males or all females. Most dances also involve moving in a circle. This circular motion symbolizes an unbreakable connection to family and its traditions. Kids as young as three years old take part in competitions, and prizes are awarded to the best performers.

Native American songs and dances tell stories. Some celebrate battles and victories; others express loss and mourning. The vibrant colors, detailed beadwork, and large feathers on outfits worn by the performers are eye catching. Clothing also plays an important role in some dances. In the "Fahay Shawl" dance, performers sway their arms so the fabric of their clothing looks like the fluttering wings of butterflies.

Fahay Shawl dance

Verna Street is a Saponi tribe member of the Cherokee Nation. She taught herself Native American dance when she was just a child. "I fell in love with the dancing at my first powwow, but no one in my family knew how to dance," she remembers. "I taught myself, through watching other people and through videos." Today, Street runs a dance studio in North Carolina so young people can learn about this Native American tradition together. "A lot of parents are busy, but they still want their children to be involved and learn the dance of their culture," she explains. "So I help them do that."[2]

Many events combine traditions from several different tribes. Ray Tahahwah, a Comanche from Oklahoma, moved to Chicago where he attended one such event. "We all have our own histories [as tribes]," he notes, "but we don't lose our [tribal] identity."[3]

Through the arts, Native Americans can preserve their heritage and create new history at the same time. Joseph Bruchac, a Native American of Abenaki descent, was raised by his grandparents in the Adirondack Mountains of New York. They provided him with a loving home, but they never spoke about their Native American ancestry.

"It was sort of the family secret," says Bruchac. "Everyone knew, but no one wanted to talk about it. The older generation tried to shield the children by not talking or emphasizing their ethnicity for fear it would hold them back."[4] Bruchac's grandfather was ridiculed at school for being Native American. He felt so unwelcome that he ended up dropping out of school in the fourth grade. He wanted his grandson to have a better life, beginning with an education.

Bruchac fulfilled his grandfather's wishes by graduating from Cornell University. When he decided to make his living as a writer, though, he turned to his heritage for inspiration. Drawn to stories about Abenaki culture, he began writing children's books with Native American themes. He has now written more than 120 books for both kids and adults. His two sons have

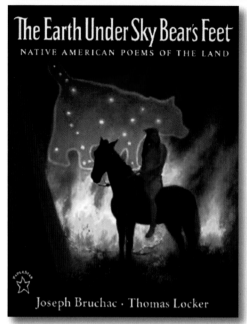

The Earth Under Sky Bear's Feet
NATIVE AMERICAN POEMS OF THE LAND

Joseph Bruchac · Thomas Locker

One of Joseph Bruchac's many books

followed in his footsteps as Native American storytellers, even co-authoring books with their father.

Jaune Quick-to-See Smith is a painter in Corrales, New Mexico. As part of the Confederated Salish and Kootenai Tribes, she feels that she has a responsibility to teach others through her art. "I see myself as an educator, teaching people about the real history of indigenous people. In our American culture today, we forget our histories and don't really look very far down the road. We all need to remember our grandparents, remember who we are and where we came from, and to pass that on to our grandchildren."[5]

While growing up in Montana, Smith often experienced racism. She remembers being called mean names by both children and adults. She and her father were even refused service in a store once because they were Native Americans. Being treated this way hurt, but she found a place for that in her work. "It gave me a place to put my thoughts," she says.[6] An amazing thing happened when she picked up a paintbrush to express herself. She was able to turn her pain into something positive, something beautiful.

Today, Smith is one of the best-known Native American artists in the Southwest. Her work hangs in such galleries as the National Museum of Women in the Arts, the Smithsonian American Art Museum, and the Museum of Modern Art in New York City. She has received numerous awards and is a member of the New Mexico Women's Hall of Fame.

TRACING NATIVE AMERICAN ROOTS

Some families, especially ones from New England, have been passing down rumors for generations about having Indian princesses or other Native Americans in their family trees. When the Europeans settled in America, some of them formed relationships with Native Americans. A small number of them even married and had families.

If you think there may be a Native American in your family history, you can now find out through a simple saliva test. Mitochondrial DNA is a form of DNA that is passed to both male and female children from their mothers. There are five forms of mitochondrial DNA that exist almost entirely in individuals with Native American ancestry.

"If you have one of those types," states Dr. Thomas Roderick, "you can be almost assured that your mother's mother's mother's mother—probably going back ten generations or so, at least—was a member of some Native American tribe."[7] Roderick is a retired geneticist and former president of the Maine Genealogical Society.

Although mitochondrial DNA can only identify ethnicity from your mother's side of the family, autosomal DNA tests are now available as well. These tests examine a much larger portion of DNA, and can identify Native American ancestry, even if it's not on your mother's side.

Home test kits can be purchased online, usually for between $100 and $300. Collecting a DNA sample is easy. Simply follow the directions to swab the inside of your mouth, and then mail it to the laboratory. In about a month, you will receive your results.

Melinda Lutz Sanborn is a genealogist in New Hampshire. She adds, "In the end, there are very few people who successfully trace in the records to an Indian person of any rank, let alone a princess. But there are tremendous inroads being made with DNA."[8]

Melinda Lutz Sanborn

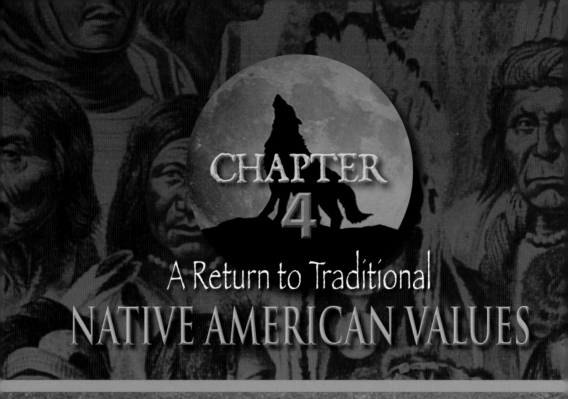

CHAPTER 4

A Return to Traditional
NATIVE AMERICAN VALUES

Interest in Native American cultures has never been stronger. Native Americans aren't the only ones who want to learn more about their traditional ways. Both Native Americans and others seem to have a deeper respect for these cultures along with an increasing desire to understand them better.

We live in a world where technology is often mistaken for progress. We communicate with each other through email and text messages. We cook our meals in microwave ovens—if we don't opt for fast food instead. Oftentimes things are valued more than people. More and more people are taking a big step back to think about what truly matters. To many of them, Native American ways make a lot of sense.

In Native American cultures, the circle is an important symbol of life. Think about standing in a circle with others. In this formation no one is first; no one is last. Each person is equal. Traditional Native Americans also see the circle as being large enough for everyone. Each person is valued, and no one is

The circle plays a major role in Native American culture. Since a circle has no beginning and no end, no one standing in the circle can be considered first or last. A circle can also grow to any size necessary to accommodate everyone and everything. It is a very welcoming symbol.

Founded in 1961, the National Indian Youth Council (NIYC) of Gallup, New Mexico, is the second-oldest national Indian organization. With thousands of members, the NIYC supports projects for Native Americans at both the local and national level.

excluded. This idea of equality is very similar to the basis of the United States Constitution.

Although the head of a tribe is often the chief, many people do not realize that Native American societies are led by councils. These groups are made up of many people who have been chosen for their experiences, insight, and humanity. Older Native Americans are respected as valuable sources of knowledge because of their vast life experience. Younger generations understand that this level of wisdom can only be achieved with time.

Younger family members also play an important part in Native American values. Like the elder members of a tribe, children are valued for their own unique traits. Laura Ramirez is the author of the book *Keepers of the Children: Native American Wisdom and Parenting.* She relays how children are valued—like fine gems—in Native American cultures. "What they say is that, when a woman is pregnant, she has a piece of turquoise inside her womb. When that piece of turquoise is born into the world, it's the parents' job—not to try to break it up, not to try to make it into something else, not to try to shape it into anything other than what it is—but to polish it until its unique beauty comes to light."[1]

Respect is a common theme in Native American cultures. Ramirez believes that respecting children teaches them tolerance. She and her husband, a Pascua Yaki tribe member, use respect to resolve conflicts with their two sons. She explains, "You do that by inviting them to consider another perspective. You do this in Native American culture by using something called the

Author Laura Ramirez believes that teaching respect and tolerance is one of the most important jobs of Native American parents today.

Talking Stick." They begin by sitting in a circle and placing the stick in the middle. "When someone feels compelled to speak, they pick up the stick. That is the sign for everyone else to be silent—not to think about what they are going to say when it is their turn to hold the stick—but to actually listen, to consider the words of the speaker, to consider this person's pain." She adds, "When you are done speaking, you put down the stick or pass it to someone else. The next person speaks. Everybody gets a chance to be listened to, and it's very important for children to be heard: to feel like they are seen, like they are visible, like their voices count."[2]

Certain museums want to show their visitors how preserving the past affects people in the present. The Tomaquag Indian Memorial Museum in Exeter, Rhode Island, is one such institution. In 2012, the museum featured an exhibit called *The Pursuit of Happiness: An Indigenous View.* This exhibit, which includes a

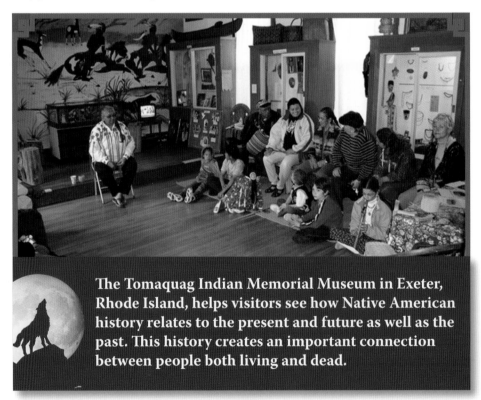

The Tomaquag Indian Memorial Museum in Exeter, Rhode Island, helps visitors see how Native American history relates to the present and future as well as the past. This history creates an important connection between people both living and dead.

The Narragansett Indian Church in Charlestown, Rhode Island, helps to preserve the culture of this northeastern tribe.

documentary film, tells the story of the tribe's efforts to reclaim its culture.

Loren Spears is a member of the Narragansett Tribal Council and the executive director of the museum. She reports, "I think that people leave here with a better understanding of our history and how it connects to us as native people today. We want them to understand that we're not talking about people dead and gone. We're talking about people here and now."[3]

The museum even offers a real school on its premise. Like other schools for children, the Nuweetooun School teaches classes like language arts, mathematics, science, social studies, and health. What makes this school different, though, is that it teaches these subjects with a focus on environmental education

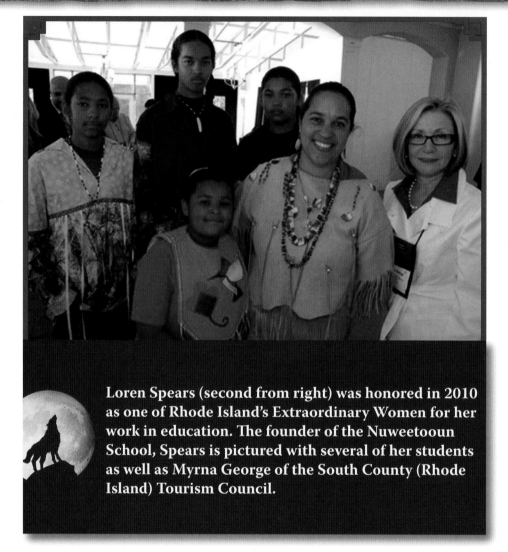

Loren Spears (second from right) was honored in 2010 as one of Rhode Island's Extraordinary Women for her work in education. The founder of the Nuweetooun School, Spears is pictured with several of her students as well as Myrna George of the South County (Rhode Island) Tourism Council.

and native culture and history. As Spears notes, the school is "teaching our children through our own cultural lens, through our cultural ideology, our own philosophy of life. We're teaching our children that it's okay to be who they are as indigenous people, and it's okay to have a different perspective on the world . . . And they need to learn the technology and to read and write and to explore the world . . . in a way that empowers them as indigenous people."[4]

A PLACE AT THE TABLE

Tocabe

Chances are good that you have never been to a Native American restaurant. If you are ever in Denver, Colorado, though, you just might get your chance. In 2008, Osage Indian Ben Jacobs opened Tocabe, an American Indian eatery, with his business partner Matthew Chandra. "I want native food to be much more in the public eye," explains Jacobs. "Feasting is a big part of our culture, and eating together is important to us, just like for many other cultures."[5]

The restaurant is named for Jacobs' mother. The word *tocabe* is the Osage word for "blue," her favorite color. It isn't just the name that she inspired, though. The food the restaurant serves is based on the recipes that she and Jacobs's grandmother made when he was growing up. After graduating from college, Jacobs and Chandra spent two years perfecting the dishes before opening the business together.

The restaurant features unique but simple dishes. One popular choice is sage-rubbed bison ribs with blueberry barbeque sauce. Another favorite menu item is Tocabe's fry bread with hominy salsa.

So far, the business has been a huge success. In 2011, Guy Fieri featured Tocabe on his Food Network television show *Diners, Drive-Ins and Dives*. Since the restaurant opened, Jacobs and Chandra have doubled their workforce, and business quadrupled one month after the Food Network appearance.

With the money they have made, Jacobs and Chandra have already provided three scholarships to Native Americans. They are also helping to educate their customers about what it means to be Native American in the twenty-first century. Some people were surprised when they held a Native hip-hop night. Jacobs shares, "We live in the modern era, too. I think sometimes we are pigeonholed into the long-hair-and-war-paint stereotype. We are trying to show that we can stay traditional in many aspects of our lives, but be just as contemporary as the rest of the people in others."[6]

CHAPTER
5
From the Past and Present
INTO THE FUTURE

In order for Native American heritage to survive, tribe members must find a way to keep the old ways alive in the changing twenty-first century. Higher education plays an important role in this process. The American Indian College Fund provides scholarships to Native Americans who want to create brighter futures for both themselves and their communities by earning degrees. The organization awards about six thousand scholarships each year.

Richard B. Williams is the president and CEO of the American Indian College Fund. He states, "American Indians are at a disadvantage financially when planning for college due to high levels of poverty and unemployment on Indian reservations, making it even more important that Native peoples plan their resources carefully."[1] To increase chances for success, the fund has produced a set of four handbooks that can be downloaded at its website. They offer advice about everything from making the first step—deciding to go to college—to getting financial aid

If Native American heritage is to be preserved, young people must first be able to take care of themselves and their families. Education allows young Native Americans to better their lives so that they can then focus on keeping their customs and languages alive.

The Native American Summer Bridge Institute (NASBI) offers Native American high school students a chance to sample the college experience. This summer camp program allows high school juniors to visit Texas Tech University for a five-day stay. While there, the students attend college classes and participate in campus activities.

and managing money. They also include stories of other Native Americans who have gone through the process already.

"We are thrilled to have the support of the National Endowment for Financial Education, with whom we collaborated to develop these important tools that can help Natives successfully navigate the road to getting into college from a financial standpoint," says Williams. "Wise financial planning is integral to getting into and staying in college to ensure students' academic and career success."[2]

Improving life on the reservations means bringing more money and jobs into these areas. Some reservations have opened casinos as a way of doing this. The Foxwoods Resort and Casino is one of the most popular of these attractions. Located on the Mashantucket Pequot Reservation in Connecticut, Foxwoods offers gaming, food, music and comedy performances, golf, a spa, and shopping.

Visiting a reservation is also a great way to learn more about Native American cultures. Tourism is a large part of the economy on many reservations, and each part of the country offers a unique experience. The largest reservation in all of North America is Navajo Nation. It includes land in three different states: northeastern Arizona, southeastern Utah, and northwestern New Mexico. Visitors can tour the rugged landscape on foot, on horseback, or in four-wheel-drive vehicles. At night they can even sleep in a hogan, a traditional Navajo home built from wooden poles, tree bark, and mud.

The Alligator Alley Reservation in southern Florida offers visitors a glimpse into life as a Miccosukee tribe member. Guests can attend cooking and craft workshops, take boat tours of the Everglades, and participate in tribal festivals. As the name of the reservation implies, the tribe shares the land with numerous alligators, which are also featured in some of the demonstrations.

Only one reservation remains in the state of Alaska. It is the Metlakatla Indian Community on Annette Island, off the southeast coast. It is home to the Tsimshian Tribe, which includes four clans called the Eagle, the Raven, the Wolf, and the Killer Whale.

Alligator in Alligator Alley

Annette Island

Other, smaller tribes also reside on the reservation. The community welcomes anyone who wants to learn about its heritage to participate in traditional activities and customs.

The symbol of the circle is fitting here as well. The more people who want to step into the circle to learn about Native American cultures, the better off the tribes will be. Some visitors may be rediscovering their own heritage. Others may simply want to learn about the tribes that lived here long before their own ancestors arrived. Either way, this interest can help create a better economy for the reservations.

In 2011, President Barack Obama said, "I believe that one day, we're going to be able to look back on these years and say that this was a turning point. This was the moment when we began to build a strong middle class in Indian Country; the moment when businesses, large and small, began opening up in reservations; the moment when we stopped repeating the mistakes of the past, and began building a better future together, one that honors old traditions and welcomes every Native American into the American Dream."[3]

NATIVE AMERICAN HERITAGE MONTH

Established by President George Bush in 1990, November is Native American Heritage Month in the United States. During these four weeks every fall, Americans are encouraged to learn more about Native American cultures. During this time, you can check out the books and videos on this subject that are showcased at many local libraries. You may also find some interesting documentaries about Native American history on television in November.

In 2011, Big Brothers Big Sisters decided to utilize Native American Heritage Month as a time to start a new campaign. The goal: to enroll more youth and volunteers from the Native American community. The campaign featured an ad from professional women's basketball player Tahnee Robinson. A Native American who grew up on the Wind River Reservation in Fort Washakie, Wyoming, she was one of the first Native Americans ever selected in the WNBA draft. Robinson wholeheartedly believes in the project. "Mentoring is about putting a child on a path to success and giving kids the power to believe that they can achieve their dreams."[4]

Ivy Wright-Bryan is the Big Brothers Big Sisters of America Director of Native American Mentoring. She is also a member of the Pyramid Lake Paiute Tribe in Nevada. She states, "By providing these specialized mentoring services, Big Brothers Big Sisters is supporting educational and community efforts that help Native American young people develop tribal, national, and international leadership skills."[5]

Heritage Month performance

Chapter 1

1. Omniglot, "Navajo (Diné Bizaad)," http://www.omniglot. com/writing/navajo.htm
2. National Archives, "Native American Heritage," http://www. archives.gov/research/native-americans/
3. Cultural Survival, "Endangered Languages: Revitalizing Native American Languages," http://www.culturalsurvival.org/ programs/elc/program?gclid=CLTI4cydnLICFUfd4Aod6VUA Mw
4. Tom Nugent, *Chicago Tribune,* "Experts Speak Out to Save Midwestern Tribal Tongues," October 12, 2003, p. 1.27.
5. David Braun, *National Geographic,* "Preserving Native America's Vanishing Languages," November 15, 2009.
6. Ibid.

Chapter 2

1. Elizabeth Norton, *Science Now,* "Starbucks of Ancient America?," August 6, 2012.
2. Bobby Lake-Thom, *Spirits of the Earth: A Guide to Native American Nature Symbols, Stories, and Ceremonies* (New York: Plume, 1997), p. 92.
3. The Official Website of the Navajo Code Talkers, "The Code Talker Story," http://www.navajocodetalkers.org/code_talker_story/

Chapter 3

1. National Park Service, "Tribal Preservation Program," http:// www.nps.gov/history/thpo/
2. Marwa Eltagouri, *McClatchy-Tribune Business News,* "Native Americans Keep Traditions Alive at Pow Wow," July 16, 2012.
3. Wilson Ring, *Chicago Tribune,* "Pow Wows Preserving A Heritage," July 1, 1991.
4. Christina Gostomski, *The Morning Call,* "Native American Turns His Heritage Into Stories," September 18, 2000.
5. Aurelio Sanchez, *Albuquerque Journal,* "Artist Ensures Beauty Has Message," May 25, 2008.

6. Ibid.
7. Meredith Goad, *The Portland Press Herald,* "DNA May Fill in Blanks for Genealogy Enthusiasts," February 27, 2005.
8. Ibid.

Chapter 4

1. "Peace Talks: Peaceful Parenting (Part 3)," KUNM Radio, July 28, 2006, http://www.goodradioshows.org/peaceTalksL41.html
2. Ibid.
3. Tom Meade, *The Providence Journal,* "Native American Pathways," January 26, 2012.
4. Ibid.
5. Amanda Bower, *Time,* "Good Old American Cooking—the Way the Native Americans Used to Make," October 27, 2011. http://www.time.com/time/nation/article/0,8599,2098045,00.html
6. Ibid.

Chapter 5

1. PR Newswire, "National Endowment for Financial Education Collaborates with American Indian College Fund to Provide Online Financial Education for Native Students," March 8, 2011.
2. Ibid.
3. The White House, "President Obama and the Native American Community," http://www.whitehouse.gov/nativeamericans
4. PR Newswire, "Big Brothers Big Sisters Celebrates Native American Heritage Month With Efforts to Expand Culturally Relevant Mentoring Services," November 1, 2011.
5. Ibid.

Brennan, Kristine. *Native Americans.* Broomall, Pennsylvania: Mason Crest Publishers, 2009.

Bruchac, Joseph. *Sacajawea.* Boston, Massachusetts: Harcourt, 2000.

Johansen, Bruce E., Ph.D. *Native Americans Today: A Biographical Dictionary.* Santa Barbara, California: Greenwood, 2010.

On the Internet

National Archives: "Native American Heritage"
http://www.archives.gov/research/native-americans/

National Museum of the American Indian
http://nmai.si.edu/home/

Works Consulted

Bower, Amanda. "Good Old American Cooking—the Way the Native Americans Used to Make." *Time,* October 27, 2011. http://www.time.com/time/nation/article/0,8599,2098045,00.html

Braun, David. "Preserving Native America's Vanishing Languages." *National Geographic,* November 15, 2009.

Brown, Joseph Epes. *Teaching Spirits: Understanding Native American Religious Traditions.* New York: Oxford University Press, 2001.

Cultural Survival: "Endangered Languages: Revitalizing Native American Languages"
http://www.culturalsurvival.org/programs/elc/program?gclid=CLTI4cydnLICFUfd4Aod6VUAMw

Eltagouri, Marwa. "Native Americans Keep Traditions Alive at Pow Wow." *McClatchy-Tribune Business News,* July 16, 2012.

Garbarino, Merwyn S., and Sasso, Robert F. *Native American Heritage.* Prospect Heights, Ill: Waveland Press, 1994.

Goad, Meredith. "DNA May Fill in Blanks for Genealogy Enthusiasts." *The Portland Press Herald,* February 27, 2005.

Gostomski, Christina. "Native American Turns His Heritage Into Stories." *The Morning Call,* September 18, 2000.

Lake-Thom, Bobby. *Spirits of the Earth: A Guide to Native American Nature Symbols, Stories, and Ceremonies.* New York: Plume, 1997.

Linthicum, Leslie. "Preserving Native Cultures." *Albuquerque Journal,* October 15, 1996.

Meade, Tom. "Native American Pathways." *The Providence Journal,* January 26, 2012.

National Archives: "Native American Heritage" http://www.archives.gov/research/native-americans/

National Park Service: "Tribal Preservation Program" http://www.nps.gov/history/thpo/

Navajo People—The Diné: "Navajo Homes—Hogans" http://navajopeople.org/navajo-hogans.htm

Norton, Elizabeth. "Starbucks of Ancient America?" *Science Now,* August 6, 2012.

Nugent, Tom. "Experts Speak Out to Save Midwestern Tribal Tongues." *Chicago Tribune,* October 12, 2003, p. 1.27.

The Official Website of the Navajo Code Talkers: "The Code Talker Story" http://www.navajocodetalkers.org/code_talker_story/

Omniglot: "Navajo (Diné Bizaad)" http://www.omniglot.com/writing/navajo.htm

"Peace Talks: Peaceful Parenting (Part 3)." KUNM Radio, July 28, 2006. http://www.goodradioshows.org/peaceTalksL41.html

PR Newswire. "Big Brothers Big Sisters Celebrates Native American Heritage Month With Efforts to Expand Culturally Relevant Mentoring Services." November 1, 2011.

PR Newswire. "National Endowment for Financial Education Collaborates with American Indian College Fund to Provide Online Financial Education for Native Students." March 8, 2011.

Ring, Wilson. "Pow Wows Preserving A Heritage." *Chicago Tribune,* July 1, 1991.

Sanchez, Aurelio. "Artist Ensures Beauty Has Message." *Albuquerque Journal,* May 25, 2008.

Tomaquag Indian Memorial Museum: "Brief History" http://www.tomaquagmuseum.com/

The White House: "President Obama and the Native American Community" http://www.whitehouse.gov/nativeamericans

archaeology (ahr-kee-OL-uh-jee): the scientific study of humans of the past through the study of their remains, architecture, and other materials

architecture (AHR-ki-tek-cher): the profession and study of designing buildings or spaces

casino (kuh-SEE-noh): a building used for entertainment, especially gambling

ethnicity (eth-NIS-i-tee): a common racial, national, tribal, religious, linguistic, or cultural origin or background

etymology (et-uh-MOL-uh-jee): the origin of a word

genetics (juh-NET-iks): the study of traits inherited through genes

grant (GRANT): a sum of money given to a person or group for a specific purpose

immunity (ih-MYOO-ni-tee): the state of being insusceptible to an illness or disease

indigenous (in-DIJ-uh-nuhs): originating in a particular region

linguist (ling-GWIST): a person who studies the science of languages

nomad (NOH-mad): a person who moves from place to place with no permanent home

racism (REY-siz-uhm): hatred or intolerance of people belonging to another race

reservation (rez-er-VEY-shuhn): a piece of land set apart for use by a particular group, such as an Indian tribe

stereotype (STER-ee-uh-tahyp): a simplified impression of an entire group of people or things based on inaccurate or a small amount of information

Navajo house called a hogan